131
Creative Conversations
For Families

Christ-honoring conversation starters to
strengthen your family bond.

Jed Jurchenko

www.CoffeeShopConversations.com

© 2016 by Jed Jurchenko.

Scripture quoted by permission.
All scripture quotations,
unless otherwise indicated,
are taken from the NET Bible®
copyright ©1996-2006
by Biblical Studies Press, L.L.C.
All rights reserved.

Printed by CreateSpace,
An Amazon.com Company
Available from Amazon.com

Creative, Christ-honoring,
conversation starters to help your family
grow closer than ever before!

Also By Jed

Find these and other great books by Jed at
www.CoffeeShopConversations.com/Books

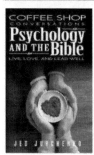

Get Free Books

To thank you for your purchase, I would like to send you a bonus gift.

Transform from discouraged and burned out, to an enthusiastic agent of joy who parents at a higher–happier–level. *Be Happier Now*, provides ten, easy to apply, happiness strategies for reducing stress and increasing joy at home!

I will also make sure that you are the first to know about free books and future deals!

www.coffeeshopconversations.com/happiness/

Dedication

To my wife, Jenny, and daughters Mackenzie, Brooklyn, Addison, and Emmalynn. You add an overwhelming amount of joy to my life. Thank you for filling our family with fun, funny, engaging, and Christ-honoring conversations. I love you all like crazy!

Contents

*** 131 Creative Conversations ***

Introduction
The Power of Conversation

The average family spends less than eight hours together each week. Sadly, much of this time is squandered in front of televisions, computers, and on smartphones — all activities where minimal engagement is required. This book is for families who long to be above average by diving into deep, meaningful, and life-changing conversations. As we will see, active engagement is essential. Time-tested, parenting wisdom, as well as the latest scientific research, both point to the value of a strong family bond.

It has been said that rules without relationship will drive children toward rebellion. Sadly, in my twenty plus years of working with families, I have seen this to be true. On the other hand, I have also watched children and teens turn their lives around after reestablishing a bond with their parents. In fact, some teens have told me that they choose to follow the rules, not out of a fear of potential consequences, but because they cannot stand the thought of breaking their mom's or dad's heart.

I know of a mother with two sons who are well into their teens. These athletic boys surpass their mom in strength and agility. Since their mom is no longer physically capable of making them do anything, these young men could easily run the show at home.

Nevertheless, it is clear that Mom is in charge. While this mother loves her sons and has a tender side to her, she is no pushover either. If needed, she is able to bring her sons to tears with only a disappointed look. This mother possesses the magical influence that flows out of a strong bond.

The best leaders expand their influence through tightly-knit relationships. The good news is that this type of powerful influence is available to every parent. However, it requires time and effort to nurture it into existence. The 131 questions in this book are designed to help you build a tender, yet influential bond at home.

Would You Rather?

Have you ever played the game *Would You Rather*? It is a relationship building game where players are forced to choose between two absurd options. Examples include:

- Would you rather have a pencil sharpening bellybutton, or a ketchup dispensing nostril?

- Would you rather wear a snowsuit in the desert, or wear a swimsuit during a snowstorm?

This brings me to the original would you rather question. It has been around for ages and goes like this, "Would you rather spend 'quality time' or 'quantity time' with someone that you love?"

This question creates a conundrum because our hearts long for both. I think back to my relationship with my wife, Jenny, and how these two ingredients immediately added value to our relationship. The two of us met on a blind date. After eating at a tiny pizzeria with a gorgeous view of San Diego Bay, I asked Jenny if she was up for a walk. She said, "Yes." Regrettably, I did not remind Jenny to bring a jacket. It was late March, and although the weather was warm, the air cooled down quickly once the sun set.

As we strolled along the shore, I noticed Jenny shivering. I suggested turning back. "No, I'm fine," she gently replied. I glanced at Jenny again and saw goosebumps running up her arms. I suggested turning around a second time, but Jenny insisted that we keep walking.

Months after our engagement Jenny finally admitted that she had been freezing. Of course, I already knew this—it was obvious! Even so, Jenny's insistence that we continue our walk meant a lot to me. Jenny wanted to spend time with me more than she wanted to get warm. This simple act of kindness increased our "quantity time" together, and as a result, we had many high-quality interactions. Like coffee and chocolate, "quality time" and "quantity time" complement each other. These two powerful forces often mean more to the people we care about than we realize.

When we love someone a few moments together is never enough. My children continually remind me of this. On busy days, I will intentionally pause my schedule to give the girls a few minutes of uninterrupted, quality time. Then, I dive back into work. Usually, it is not long before my four daughters are again clamoring for attention — and why shouldn't they? I am the one who made the mistake of thinking that quality time was sufficient. When it comes to the "quality time" versus "quantity time" debate, settling on one is impossible. Our hearts long for both!

Quantity Time's Vanishing Act

Like a skilled magician, quantity time has performed a vanishing act, and quality time is following close behind. Families are busier than ever before. One side effect of technology is that work can now hunt us down. Last minute emails and internet projects are quickly becoming a new norm. As a result, connecting as a family requires intentionality and effort.

For me personally, the days seem to fly by. It is as if someone pressed the fast-forward button on life! I suspect that many parents can relate. There are simply not enough hours in the day to accomplish everything that needs to be done.

As a society, we are perfecting the art of efficiency by learning to accomplish more in less time. Although this is great for the bottom-line at work, when productivity tools invade our homes, relationships suffer. A decrease in the amount of time spent together will also diminish the number of quality family interactions. Quality time and quantity time simply cannot be separated.

The Power of Time

In 1930, British economist John Keynes predicted the world was moving toward a fifteen-hour workweek. He suggested that in the future, humanities most significant challenge would be finding ways to occupy their abundance of free time.

Unfortunately, Keynes prediction never came to fruition. In fact, the opposite happened. In 2014, Gallup's Work and Education Survey reported that the average workweek increased from 40 hours a week to 47 hours. Uninterrupted family time is declining — which is a problem that this book seeks to resolve!

Diminishing Connections

It is easy to fall into the trap of replacing connections with convenience. This is something that we are guilty of doing in our own home. Let me explain with a real-life example:

Growing up, a family movie night was a big deal. My dad, brother, and I would race to the car and drive to the nearest video rental store. After selecting a movie, we would stop for popcorn or Carne Asada fries before returning home. Quality time and quantity time were required for every family movie night.

Contrast this with our home today. Thanks to online video streaming, when our family wants to rents a movie, we turn on our television, push a few buttons, and make a selection. Although there may be a brief discussion — or debate — about what we are going to watch, there is little engagement beyond this. This is one small example of the many subtle ways that our world is trading connection for convenience.

Quality and Quantity Connections

Life's grandest adventures begin with ordinary events. During a rainy-day game of hide-and-seek, Lucy opens the wardrobe and discovers the land of Narnia. After a long day at home, Harry Potter sulkily enters his room. He finds a mischievous house elf, by the name of Dobby, sitting on his bed, and the adventures begin. Alice lays drowsily by the riverbank, bored by the book her sister is reading, just moments before falling down the rabbit hole. It is during the stretches of quantity time together — often the ones that start in a dull and insignificant manner — that adventures find us!

The magical delights that fill our favorite books are not reserved for fairy tales. Last week, I spent the majority of the day with Addison, our almost-two-year-old. Jenny is in the process of opening a daycare and needed the two of us to vacate the house. She had reached the maximum capacity for toddlers and received another request for care. Rather than decline a family in need, Jenny and I agreed that I would take Addison on an extended daddy-daughter date.

To prepare, I loaded the baby-backpack into our mini-van, along with a few bottles of water, and some snacks. The two of us spent the morning at a playground, followed by a hike on the beach in the afternoon. Addison and I had a blast exploring tide-pools, splashing in the waves, and eating junk food.

That evening, while Jenny and I were looking at pictures of our outing, Jenny pointed out that Addison was beaming. Her smile stretched from ear to ear in every photo. This impromptu day of goofing-off became a highlight of our week. Quality interactions are a byproduct of quantity time. When families spend time together, quality interactions naturally follow.

Jump-Starting Family Time

The goal of this book is twofold. The first objective is to support your family in strengthening your relationships with Christ-honoring conversations that require both quality and quantity time. The second objective is to encourage your family to ask good questions. It is astounding how much we parents learn about our children when we ask the right questions. In short, the goal of this book is to help you jump-start meaningful family time together!

How to Get The Most From This Book

Chapter 1 outlines three foundational tools, from psychology and the Bible, for getting the most out of your family interactions—however long or short these moments may be. The remainder of the book requires the participation of the entire family.

The 131 questions in the pages ahead are divided into thirteen sections. Each chapter begins with an introduction to a key value. Read the introductions aloud, and then dive into the questions that hone-in on each value. Although a few conversation starters consist of a single question, most of them include follow-up questions that encourage your family to dive deeper into the discussion.

As you make your way through this book, allow the conversations to flow. Skip over questions that are not a good fit. Create your own follow-up questions and, most of all, have fun!

Asking and Listening

As a marriage and family therapist who has spent the past six years working with families in crisis, one of the biggest mistakes that I have watched adults make is being far too eager to speak and equally as slow to listen. When children misbehave, the initial reaction is to correct and lecture. When this happens, it only takes a few moments for children's eyes to glaze over. Physically they are present, but mentally they are on another planet. During these one-sided discourses, little learning takes place. Perhaps this is why James 1:19 says, "Let every person be quick to listen, slow to speak, slow to anger." This is sound advice that both parents and children would be wise to follow!

Today, therapists are learning to use a tool called motivational interviewing to create life-changing conversations. This form of therapy begins with the client talking and the therapist drawing him or her out with active listening. The agenda is to hear the other person's story. Moving toward change comes later.

When a car is traveling in the wrong direction, making a U-turn is easy. When a vehicle is stuck in the mud, getting it moving again is difficult. Similarly, instilling positive values in our children is much easier when our children engage. Two-way conversations can be tactfully steered down a favorable route, but talking to a tuned-out child goes nowhere.

I suggest that parents adopt an approach similar to what motivational interviewers use. Listen to your family. Ask questions that encourage your children to share their inner world. After you have listened thoroughly — and only then — share, teach, and instruct.

Two Surprises of Listening

Attentive listening brings two gifts. First, is the gift of learning. I am always amazed at how much I find out about my children when I take the time to listen. I will share a story about this in the next chapter. Second is the gift of being heard. Begin with a lecture and your family will tune you out. Start with listening — the intense listening that can almost be felt — and you may be surprised at how engaged your family becomes when it is your turn to talk.

In the next chapter, we will dive into three tools to help you level-up your listening skills. I wish you many happy conversations in the pages ahead!

Sincerely,

COFFEE SHOP CONVERSATIONS

Conversations and Chocolate-Chips

Three Tools for Listening Deeply

What do psychology, chocolate-chips, popcorn, and a five-year-old have in common? Apparently, a lot! In the 1960's, psychology took a giant leap forward with Carl Rogers and his formation of person-centered therapy. Before this, therapists were impersonal. Their job was to remain a "blank slate." Therapists would sit behind their clients to hide their reactions. It was erroneously believed that therapists could best help their clients by interpreting the client's experiences while interjecting as little of their personality as possible.

Then, Carl Rogers changed everything. In person-centered therapy, therapists give up the role of expert and treat their clients as equals. Instead of hiding their feelings, therapists are congruent; meaning their feelings on the inside match their emotions on the outside. Today, we call this being real.

Under Rogers' tutelage, therapists became empathetic listeners. They learned to demonstrate unconditional positive regard-- or to believe in their client's and desire the best for them no matter what.

Carl believed that empathy, congruence, and unconditional positive regard are the necessary and sufficient conditions for constructive change. These three ingredients create a magical environment where growth happens naturally. Empathy, congruence, and unconditional positive regard are not only outstanding tools for therapists, but they are also powerful tools for parents who want to develop a life-long connection with their kids.

Empathy, congruence, and unconditional positive regard are the building blocks of healthy relationships. In families, these qualities create a safe haven where children feel free to talk about errors in judgment before things get out of hand. These are the ideal skills to practice as you make your way through this book. On a personal note, whenever I put empathy, congruence, and unconditional positive regard into practice in my own home, I am always delighted by the results.

Chocolate-Chips Connection

It was an exceptionally busy Thursday. I woke up with my mind racing, wondering how I was going to survive the onslaught of activities headed our way. In addition to a full day of work, there were also the children's piano lessons and two open houses to attend. Further complicating matters was the fact that the open houses were at different schools and scheduled at precisely the same time.

To top this off, Brooklyn, our-five-year-old, had a minimum day at school. This meant less time for work and more schedule juggling for Jenny and myself. I still get a nervous twitch when I think back to all the business. Fortunately, on this particular day, this massive muddle of activity collided to form a masterpiece. Here is how things worked out:

That afternoon, Jenny dropped Brooklyn off at home and raced to take care of some errands. I was in the middle of a big project at work and needed to focus. Thinking quickly, I pulled a craft for Brooklyn out of our art bin. Brooklyn happily engaged in her activity, while I typed. After finishing the most urgent work projects, I paused for a break. Brooklyn and I microwaved a bag of popcorn, and we added in a hand-full of chocolate-chips for fun.

During our break, I gave Brooklyn my undivided attention. She shared about her day at school, talked about her new friends, and other important stuff in her five-year-old world. I am always amazed at how much she shares when I take the time to listen. After about fifteen minutes it was time to get back to work. The rest of the day was a whirlwind of activity.

Here is the best part. At one point—while our family was racing from one school to the next—I overheard Brooklyn tell her sister, "Kenzie, today daddy and I had special time together. We made popcorn and ate chocolate chips... and it was the best popcorn ever!" In the midst of our chaotic day, this simple moment of joy had made all the difference!

Small moments of joy with our children make a lasting impression on their hearts. Brooklyn's words remind me that being present, and listening with undivided attention, is a powerful parenting tool. Of course, popcorn and chocolate chips help too!

It is easy to get so caught up in the events of the day that we forget to connect with our children. I am guilty of this more often than I would like to admit. On this particular day, I was fortunate enough to get things right. The 131 conversation starters in the chapters ahead are an invitation to step out of the hustle and bustle of life and step into your child's inner world. You may be surprised at how much you learn and be pleased with how much your child takes to heart the wisdom you share!

131
Christ-Honoring Conversations For Families

Ask the right questions if you're going to find the right answers.

~Vanessa Redgrave

Counsel in a person's heart is like deep water, but an understanding person draws it out.

~ Proverbs 20:5

Fun Conversation Starters

Families are like fudge — mostly sweet, with a few nuts.

~ Anonymous

Family camping trips, goofy games of charades, popcorn and movie nights, and long days at the beach. These are a few of my happy childhood memories.

Today, Jenny and I strive to create a culture of joy and playfulness in our home. From nerf-gun fights to silly stories, and bonfires before bedtime, fun is a cherished family value.

Nevertheless, we don't engage in these activities just because we enjoy them. Having fun is serious business. It has been said that the family who plays together, stays together. Fun is so essential that the renowned therapist William Glasser included it on his list of five basic human needs.

On a similar note, Proverbs 17:22 says, "A cheerful heart is good medicine." Laughter, fun, and a spirit of playfulness are remedies that heal festering wounds. Having fun together strengthens family unity and is the foundation on which life-long, happy memories are built.

After the kids are grown, you will never hear a parent say, "I spent too much time enjoying my children." Instead, these happy family moments become the most cherished memories of all.

As you can see, having fun really is serious business. The following questions are designed to help your family foster a spirit of fun and outrageous-joy in your home!

Conversation #1

If you could have any superpower, what would it be? How would you use this power to serve others? How would you use it to help yourself?

Conversation #2

If you could spend a day with any fictional character, who would it be, and why?

Conversation #3

Describe what your perfect day looks like. Pretend there are no rules and money is not an issue. Where would you go, what would you do, and who would you bring with you?

Conversation #4

If you could take a vacation anywhere in the world, where would you travel, and why?

Conversation #5

If you chose a theme song for your life, what would it be? What about this song resonates with you?

Conversation #6

Imagine you are asked to put together the best dinner ever. What food would you put on the menu?

Conversation #7

What is one of your all-time favorite books? What do you like best about it? How has this book caused you to think or act differently?

Conversation #8

Would you rather be able to fly or be able to breathe underwater? Why?

Conversation #9

Who is the real-life hero that you admire most? What are some of this person's best qualities?

Conversation #10

What are some of life's simple pleasures that make you smile and laugh? When is the last time that you engaged in one of these activities?

Gritty Conversations

Grit is the ability to press forward when life gets difficult. It's a quality demonstrated by Daniel, one of my favorite Biblical heroes. Daniel was a captive in a foreign land, and to make matters worse, the king issued a decree stating no one could pray to anyone but him. Those who disobeyed were ordered to be thrown into a den of lions.

In spite of the danger, Daniel continued to pray, with gritty persistence, three times a day. If you don't know what happens next, you'll want to read the full story found in the book of Daniel. You will hear about how God honored Daniel's faithfulness by performing an incredible miracle! Gritty Christians remain faithful to Christ during the storms of life.

Angela Duckworth is another leader who understands the value of grit. Angela is a psychology professor who specializes in the connection of grit to long-term success. Before this, Angela taught math. She noticed that it wasn't the brightest students who did the best in her classes but the ones who worked the hardest.

Gritty people approach life like a marathon. They know that getting off to a speedy start is not nearly as important as finishing the race. Gritty people push themselves when life gets difficult.

Angela discovered that gritty students do better in college. Her research revealed that student with grit, and not the ones with the highest IQ's, are the ones who are most likely to graduate with honors.

Angela defines grit as, "Sticking with things over the very long term until you master them." Galatians 6:9 says, "We must not grow weary in doing good, for in due time we will reap, if we do not give up." Both the Bible and science affirm that grit is a valuable quality to possess.

In this chapter, you will find conversation starters designed to foster a spirit of grit in your home!

Conversation #11

Imagine a close friend is failing a class at school and comes to you for advice. What study tips and wisdom would you offer?

Conversation #12

When you have a problem that is too big to tackle on your own, which friends and family members can turn to for help? What made you choose these people?

Conversation #13

What is one big goal that you would like to accomplish in the future? What specific actions are you taking to reach your goal?

Conversation #14

What is one challenge you are currently facing? How are you working to overcome this difficulty? How can your friends and family support you along the way?

Conversation #15

If you get discouraged and stop moving toward your goals, how could your family encourage you?

Conversation #16

For kids: If you were being bullied at school, what would you do?

For Parents: Is there a time you were bullied? How did you manage the situation? Do you think you handled it well, or do you wish you had done things differently?

Conversation #17

Do you know someone who is being picked on? What steps can you take to encourage them? How can help prevent the bullying from happening again?

Conversation #18

Do you believe that it is ever OK to get into a physical fight? If so, when? What strategies should someone try before fighting?

Conversation #19

Imagine your friend has some significant problems and feels overwhelmed. What advice would you give your friend to help him or her feel less stressed? What things do you do to manage stress well?

Conversation #20

Who do you know that is exceptionally good at overcoming difficulties? What qualities does this person have that keeps him or her going?

Love Conversations

Family is where life begins
and love never ends.

~ Anonymous

Love is the key ingredient in every good fairytale. Love inspires the prince to overcome impossible odds to rescue his princess, and love is the reason that the two live happily ever after. Yet, love is not reserved for fantasies. The yearning to love and to be loved burns within every heart. Without love we are incomplete.

In Matthew 5:44, Jesus proclaims the value of love by declaring it the greatest Biblical command of all time. "Love God, and love people," this is the foundation of the Old Testament laws — all 613 of them!

The longing for love is the theme of songs, books, and movies. Yet, in spite of all of the attention it receives, love is frequently misunderstood. Love is much more than a pleasant feeling. In fact, sometimes, love does not feel warm and fuzzy at all.

I once heard love defined as doing the next right thing for someone else. Sometimes the next right thing feels great—like when we give our family gifts on their birthday, or when a best friend stays at our house for a sleepover. At other times, love is hard—like when parents have to take their children to the doctor or dentist for shots and fillings their children don't want, to keep them healthy!

Loving our friends when they are nice is easy. When life gets messy, loving others is more difficult. It takes wisdom to love well.

This is true because God does not expect us to love people only when it is easy. We are called to love others the way that God does—all of the time! The following questions are designed to stir up conversations about the easy and the challenging aspects of love and to help you nurture a spirit of loving kindness in your home!

Conversation #21

What do you think it means to love someone? How do you know when someone loves you?

Conversation #22

What have you done this week to show your family that you love them? If you can't think of anything, what will you do later this week?

Conversation #23

In his book, *The Five Love Languages*, Gary Chapman identifies quality time, physical touch, words of affirmation, gifts, and acts of service as ways that people demonstrate love to others. Which of these love languages is the easiest for you to speak?

Conversation #24

Quality time, physical touch, words of affirmation, gifts, and acts of service are also different ways that people receive love. Which love language makes you feel the most valued? What does it feel like when someone speaks your love language?

Conversation #25

John 13:35 says "Everyone will know by this that you are my disciples–if you have love for one another." What are some ways that you show love to the people around you?

Conversation #26

In Matthew 5:44 Jesus said, "Love your enemy and pray for those who persecute you." What are some ways that you can show love to your enemies?

Conversation #27

Who is someone in your life that is difficult to love? How will you show loving-kindness toward this person this week?

Conversation #28

How will you know (or how did you know) that you have fallen in love?

Conversation #29

How do you treat someone (or how should you treat someone) when you are out on a date?

Conversation #30

What do you think a good first date looks like? At what age do you think that boys and girls should begin to date?

Happiness Conversations

When one door of happiness closes, another opens, but often we look so long at the closed door that we do not see the one that has been opened for us.

~ Helen Keller

As a daddy to four girls, one of my simple joys in life is returning home after a long day at work. As I step through our front door, my girls squeal with delight, "Daddy's home." Their joy always brings a smile to my face, and no matter how exhausted I am, I instantly feel recharged!

Happiness is contagious. The downside is that grumpiness and sorrow—much like a bad cold—are highly infectious. Our moods matter because they rub off on everyone we meet. The good news is that our moods don't happen by accident. We can influence how we feel and to choose what attitude we will spread. The only question is whether we will decide to spread sourness or joy.

Proverbs 16:20 says that happiness comes from trusting in God, and Psalm 37:4 commands believers to delight in the Lord. Happy people honor God with their joy.

Contrary to popular belief, taking care of ourselves is not selfish. Mark 1:35 tells how Jesus would wake up early to walk and pray. Jesus cared for himself so that he could care for others. You and I would be wise to follow His example.

Similar to a car, your body must be refueled to run well. Stepping out of the hustle and bustle of life, and having fun, is the best ways to recharge.

Happy people make the best leaders, parents, and friends. Yet, no one can force you to be happy. Others can shower you with kindness and do nice things for you, but none of this will make you happy. Ultimately, your happiness is your choice. The following questions will help you take charge of your happiness and further instill a spirit of joy in your home!

Conversation #31

What is one of your happiest memories? What made this time so great?

Conversation #32

List some small acts of kindness that you have done in the past for a friend or your family to brighten their day?

Conversation #33

What small acts of kindness could you do for your family this week to help make their days brighter?

Conversation #34

Think of someone you know who is feeling down. Brainstorm how you can work together, as a family, to brighten this person's day.

Conversation #35

If one of your friends or family members saw that you were sad, what are some simple things that they could do to cheer you up?

Conversation #36

Who is the happiest person that you know? What do you think makes this person so cheerful?

Conversation #37

On a scale of 1-10, with 1 being miserable, and 10 being ecstatic, how happy are you right now? Why did you choose this number? What would need to happen to raise your happiness level by one point?

Conversation #38

1 Timothy 6:6 says, "Now godliness combined with contentment brings great profit." Do you think you are a content person? Why or why not? What could you do to be more content?

Conversation #39

Do you think it is hard or easy for you to be happy? Why?

Conversation #40

What are three things that are going well for you today?

Scary Conversations

You gain strength, courage, and confidence by every experience in which you really stop to look fear in the face. You must do the thing which you think you cannot do.

~ Eleanor Roosevelt

In scary movies, the creepy things always come out at night. In real life, hiding our fears allows them to grow. Talking about the things we are afraid of brings healing and growth.

Trauma therapists help their clients to heal by talking about their pain. Fears and hurts are challenging to discuss at first, but as time goes on, the conversations become easier. Eventually, talking about the pain becomes as easy as ordering a cheeseburger at a drive-through restaurant. Not everyone needs therapy to overcome his or her fears. The bottom line is that talking about what scares us is essential.

When we shine a light on our fears by

talking about them, the less intimidating our fears become. The word *fear* occurs more than 500 times in the Bible, which means this is a topic that is important to God. The phrase *"fear not"* appears over 100 times in Scripture. This is significant because it shows us that living in fear is not God's plan.

James 5:16 says, "Confess your sins to one another and pray for one another so that you may be healed." God knows that talking about what bothers us — including sins, worries, fears, and past hurts — brings healing.

In this chapter, you will find fear based conversation starters. If you and your family find yourself diving into sensitive topics, remember to cheer each other on. Not every problem needs to be resolved right away. Sometimes, knowing that our family hears, understands, and values us is enough.

My prayer is that these fear-based conversations draw you closer than ever before!

Conversation #41

What movie frightens you? What is it about this movie that scares you the most?

Conversation #42

What are three things that scare you? Do you think these fears are realistic or do you think that you are more afraid of these things than you need to be?

Conversation #43

What are two or three things that you do to feel better when you are afraid?

Conversation #44

Who is one of the bravest people you know? What qualities does this person have that you could copy when you are afraid?

Conversation #45

Imagine that you have a friend who worries about lots of things. What advice would you give your friend to help him or her worry less?

Conversation #46

In Psalm 56:3, David writes, "When I am afraid, I trust in you." What can you do to put your trust in God when you feel scared?

Conversation #47

Do you consider yourself to be a fearful person or a brave person? Why?

Conversation #48

What are some activities that scare you that you would like to try? What would you need to do to prepare for these things?

Conversation #49

Can you think of a time in your life when fear kept you safe or out of trouble? What happened and how did fear help protect you?

Conversation #50

Is there an area of your life where fear is holding you back? What steps could you take to conquer this fear?

Money Conversations

Don't make money your goal.
Instead, pursue the things you love doing,
and then do them so well that people can't
take their eyes off you.

~Maya Angelou

1 Timothy 6:10 says, "The love of money is the root of all evils." It is true. Money — and the relentless pursuit of more money — is a recipe for all kinds of trouble.

On the other hand, money is a good thing when you are hungry, and your favorite pizza place is just around the corner. Money is regularly misunderstood. The Bible does not say that having money is wrong.

In fact, Jesus had a group of people who provided for him from their own savings — which means they had money readily available. Instead, it is the love of money that is the real problem. When money becomes more important than friends, family, and God — when greed becomes a barrier to loving the people around us — this is when the real trouble begins.

Learning to use money the right way is an ongoing process that begins with a conversation. Money is not going away any time soon. Trying to avoid the evil side of money by attempting to live without it would be an unnecessary burden--and just plain silly!

This chapter is all about learning how to use money the right way. The questions are designed to generate conversations about the good, the bad, and the ugly sides of money so that you and your family can grow in your ability to wisely use the finances that God has blessed you with!

Conversation #51

Imagine that someone gives you one million dollars. The only catch is that any money left over at the end of the day has to be returned. How would you spend your million-dollar gift?

Conversation #52

What is something that you are saving for (or would like to save for) right now? Are you doing a good job saving, and how could you save better?

Conversation #53

Imagine that there is something that you really want but can't afford. What are three things you could do to earn money toward your purchase?

Conversation #54

How do you use the money that you earn to encourage and bless others? If you are not doing this yet, what small actions will you take to start doing this?

Conversation #55

2 Corinthians 9:7 says, "God loves a cheerful giver." Do you consider yourself to be a cheerful giver? Why or why not?

Conversation #56

Do you think that your family has enough money to be truly happy right now? Why or why not? If not, how much money would it take for you to be satisfied?

Conversation #57

1 Timothy 6:10 says, "For the love of money is the root of all evils." What are some ways money is, or could become a negative influence in your life?

Conversation #58

If your friends asked you for advice about money, what wisdom would you share?

Conversation #59

What are some of the worst money decisions that you have made, and what would you do differently if you had the chance?

Conversation #60

What are some of the best decisions you have made with your money? What are some of the things you did right that made things turn out so well?

Spiritual Conversations

I believe the Bible is the best gift God has ever given to man. All the good from The Savior of the world is communicated to us through this Book.

~ *Abraham Lincoln*

When I was three years old, I made the most important decisions of my life. I prayed with my mom and asked Jesus to be my Lord and Savior. When I prayed, I had a three-year-olds understanding of what it means to follow God.

Now that I am older, I know more. I have also grown in the ways that I follow God. Walking with Christ is an ongoing journey and not a onetime event. This is why it is so important to talk about God daily.

In the Old Testament, the Israelites would write Scriptures on their doorposts, hold special feasts, and set up landmarks as reminders to include God in every aspect of their lives.

In Deuteronomy 11:18, God encourages His followers to, "Fix these words of mine into your mind and being, and tie them as a reminder on your hands and let them be symbols on your forehead."

One of the best ways to solidify God's word in your mind and heart is through conversation. The more that we talk about God, the more our understanding of how we can best follow Him, grows.

In this chapter, you will find ten spiritual conversations to encourage you and your family to keep growing in Christ!

Conversation #61

What do you think it means to be a Christian? Are you a Christian? Why, or why not?

Conversation #62

If you could travel back in time, and have lunch with one Biblical character — other than Jesus — who would you eat with, and why?

Conversation #63

If you had the opportunity to ask God one question, what would you ask Him? How do you think God would answer your question? Be sure to get feedback from your family on how they think God might answer this question too.

Conversation #64

Galatians 5:22 says, "But the fruit of the Spirit is love, joy, peace, forbearance, kindness, goodness, faithfulness, gentleness, and self-control." Which of these fruits are present in your life, and how do they show?

Conversation #65

When is a time that you prayed to God and He answered your prayer? What did you pray about, and what happened?

Conversation #66

What is one of your favorite Bible stories or verses? What makes this passage of Scripture so meaningful to you?

Conversation #67

In Mathew 5:44, Jesus tells his followers to love their enemies and pray for those who persecute them? Have you ever shown love to someone who has been mean to you? If so, what did you do? Is there someone in your life who is hurting you that you need to keep in prayer?

Conversation #68

A well-known quote says, "Preach the Gospel at all times and when necessary use words." What are some ways you are preaching God's word through your actions? What are some additional things you could start doing to spread the Gospel through your actions?

Conversation #69

What types of actions are you taking to grow closer to God? What is one thing that you would like to add to your list in the future?

Conversation #70

Is sharing your faith with your friends easy or difficult for you? What would make this easier?

Rules Conversations

Practicing the Golden Rule is not a sacrifice,
it's an investment.

~ Anonymous

In college, I worked at a summer camp for kids. The number one rule of the camp was, "You must have fun!" Every time the camp director announced this rule, all of the children would erupt into a roaring cheer. The catch, however, was that everything done at camp had to be fun for everybody.

Although punching an annoying camper in the nose might feel enjoyable for a moment, it is not much fun for the kid who was hit. Nor, is it fun when you have to deal with the consequences of punching someone—such as calling your parents to pick you up early from camp. Thus, hitting was not allowed at camp, because it was not fun for everyone.

Working at summer camp gave me a new perspective on rules. Following the rules can be fun when we understand that they protect us from getting hurt. Those who take the rules seriously are protected from adverse consequences that rule breakers receive.

Finally, abiding by the rules is another way that you and your family can honor Christ. God calls children to follow the rules their parents set. Ephesians 6:1 says, "Children, obey your parents in the Lord."

However, children are not the only ones with rules to follow. Romans 13:1 says "Let every person be subject to the governing authorities." God puts leaders in place that set standards for adults too.

In this chapter, you and your family will dive into conversations that will cause you to think deeply about the importance of rules. Who knows, you may even get excited about rules and see them in a whole new light, as I did!

Conversation #71

If you were president of the United States for a day, what rules would you change, and why?

Conversation #72

Are there any unjust laws in our world that you would like to be a part of fixing? What makes you passionate about changing these particular laws?

Conversation #73

What rules at school, work, and home do you like? Can you think of some rules that make your life better?

Conversation #74

What rules at school, work, and home do you not like? If you could change these rules, which ones would you alter, and why?

Conversation #75

Is it ever right to break the rules? If so, when is a rule okay to break?

Conversation #76

What commands in the Bible are easy for you to follow? Which ones do you need to work on?

Conversation #77

Is there a rule at home that you currently have a hard time obeying? What could you do to follow this rule better?

Conversation #78

Ephesians 6:1 says, "Children, obey your parents in the Lord for this is right." How do you think you do at following this Biblical command? How can you keep growing in this area?

Conversation #79

If you ever got in big trouble for breaking a rule and needed help, whom would you talk to first? Why?

Conversation #80

Are there any rules that you think your family should make? If so, what should they be and how would they benefit your family?

Family Conversations

Everyone needs a house to live in, but a supportive family is what builds a home.

~ Anthony Liccione

Your family is a gift from God. It is where many of your best, lifelong memories are made! Of course, your family is probably the source of some of your greatest frustrations too, but this is normal. We spend more time with our families than we do with our teachers and friends. So, it's only natural that your family will rub you the wrong way at times—and I guess that there are a few things that you do that annoy your family as well.

John 7:5 tells us that not even Jesus' own brothers believed in Him for a time. Later, they became some of his greatest fans. Thus, conflict was even a normal part of Jesus' home.

Avoiding family conflict is impossible. The important thing is to learn how to move through disagreements gracefully, and to work together to make the most of the many joyful moments that come our way!

When I was in middle school, I bought a 3D poster for my room. At first glance, the poster looked like a jumbled mess of black and green lines that crisscrossed from one end of the poster to the other. However, if you stared at it in just the right way, a 3D image of three eagles soaring high above the trees would appear.

Some of my friends had to gaze at the picture for as long as fifteen minutes before they could see it. This poster is a good metaphor for our families. Sometimes, at first glance, our families look like a mess. However, when we focus on our family long enough, and in the right ways, a beautiful picture appears.

This chapter is all about conversations that will help you explore and appreciate your beautiful, messy, God-given family!

Conversation #81

What are some of the best thing about being a part of this family?

Conversation #82

What are some of the things that make being a part of this family frustrating?

Conversation #83

What is one of your happiest memories of a time we spent together as a family? What is it that made this time so special?

Conversation #84

How do you know that your family loves you, and what are some of the simple things they do to show you their love? Which is your favorite?

Conversation #85

Which family member do you get frustrated with the most? What is one thing you could do to get along better with this family member? What is one thing this family member could do to get along better with you?

Conversation #86

How do you show love to other members of your family? What is your favorite way to serve and love your family?

Conversation #87

What family activities do you like the most?

Conversation #88

What is one of your favorite holiday memories? What makes this memory so special?

Conversation #89

What are some of the chores you do at home to help your family? Is there anything that needs to be added to this list?

Conversation #90

What specific actions will you take to encourage and support your family this week?

Adventure Conversations

Life is either a daring adventure
or nothing at all.

~ Helen Keller

You are not a mistake. God designed you for a purpose. In Psalm 139:13, David writes, "Certainly you made my mind and heart; you wove me together in my mother's womb." You are God's, one-of-a-kind, masterpiece!

Because you are God's handiwork, life is not about you. It is, however, about the one who shaped you. There is a reason God put you on earth. Although fulfilling your God-given calling may not be easy, it will also not be boring!

Following God is filled with adventure! The Bible is divided into two parts, the Old Testament and the New Testament. Much of the Old Testament focuses on God's chosen people, the nation of Israel.

The Old Testament is full of adventure. At times, the people of Israel wondered if God had given up on them. They wondered if God still loved them and was still looking over them.

In Jeremiah 29:11, God gives His answer, stating, "For I know what I have planned for you,' says the LORD. 'I have plans to prosper you, not to harm you. I have plans to give you a future filled with hope." God knows the plans he has for the nation of Israel, and God knows the plans that He has for you. God's plans are not always safe, but they are always good!

You are a unique, God-designed masterpiece. God is calling you into an adventure of following Him. These following questions are about the incredible adventure God is calling you into!

Conversation #91

What is the best adventure you ever had? What made this time so memorable?

Conversation #92

What is one adventure you would like to have in the future?

Conversation #93

What is your favorite extreme sport to watch? Would you ever try this sport yourself?

Conversation #94

Are you more likely to be adventurous or play it safe, and why?

Conversation #95

Is there a time in your life where you wish you had been more adventurous? What do you wish you did differently?

Conversation #96

What are some steps you are taking (or could take) to conquer your fears and become a braver, more adventurous person?

Conversation #97

Who is the most adventurous person you know? What qualities does this person have that you would like to copy?

Conversation #98

Is there a time in your life when you were too adventurous? What happened, and what do you wish you had done differently?

Conversation #99

What advice would you give to a friend who says that he wants to add more adventure into his life?

Conversation #100

What adventure do you think God is calling you and your family into? What steps will you take to fulfill God's calling on your life?

Career Conversations

Don't ask what the world needs. Ask what makes you come alive, and go do it. Because what the world needs is people who have come alive.

~ Howard Thurman

During my junior year of high school, my dad asked me how I would feel about getting a summer job."I would love that, but I don't know where to begin," I replied. "Well, the Zoo is putting on a hiring fair in just a few weeks. Why don't you start there?" my dad stated.

After going through three rounds of interviews, I was hired. No, I didn't get to work with the animals—that required a college education and lots more experience. My job was selling hotdogs and ice-cream cones. I made $5.25 an hour, which was more than the minimum wage, and a decent salary for a first job—at least I thought so!

I tell this story because my first job began with a conversation between my dad and I. Talking about career aspirations is important. Did you know that your Heavenly Father cares about your work too?

Colossians 3:23 says, "Whatever you are doing, work at it with enthusiasm, as to the Lord and not for people." Whether you are doing chores at home, interviewing for a first job, or are well into your career, God wants you to be an enthusiastic worker who allows His love to shine.

One of the best ways to accomplish this is to have career conversations early on. This chapter is all about the work you are doing right now and the work that God is calling you to do in the future!

Conversation #101

What career do you think would be the most fun to work? Why?

Conversation #102

What career do you think that you would enjoy the least, and why?

Conversation #103

Who is the hardest worker you know? What are some of the positive qualities this person has that you could copy?

Conversation #104

Do you think attending college is important? Why, or why not? What college might you want to attend in the future?

Conversation #105

Colossians 3:23 says, "Whatever you are doing, work at it with enthusiasm, as to the Lord and not for people." What specific actions can you take to live out this Scripture at home or at school?

Conversation #106

Are there any careers that you would not be willing to do under any circumstances? If so, which jobs would you not do and why?

Conversation #107

Do you think it is more important to choose a career that you enjoy or one that pays well? Why?

Conversation #108

Do you have any hobbies that could turn into a career or a part-time job one day? If so, what are they?

Conversation #109

What new skills or hobbies would you like to begin in the future?

Conversation #110

What character qualities do you have that will help you succeed at work or at school? How are you using these qualities right now?

Growing Conversations

When speaking on the topic of personal growth, I will hide a tiny object in my clenched fist, and ask the group to guess what I am hiding. I'll state:

This object is so small that I can hide it in my hand. Yet, it is powerful enough to split enormous boulders in two — but don't worry, it's entirely safe. It is so safe that you can sit on it, eat off it, and even eat it. In fact, you may also want to live in it.

If you guessed "a redwood tree," you are right, and the object in my hand is a redwood seed. A redwood seed is so powerful that if it begins to grow in the crack of a rock, that seed will split the boulder in two! Birds and squirrels love to eat the seeds, and lumber from redwood trees makes gorgeous furniture and homes.

In Redwood National Park, there are trees so large that you can drive your car through a tunnel carved into the tree! However, before a seed can do any of these things, it needs to grow.

Like a redwood tree, you and I are made to grow too. 2 Peter 3:18 says, "But grow in the grace and knowledge of our Lord and Savior Jesus Christ." Redwood seeds require good soil, water, fresh air, and plenty of sunlight. To grow spiritually, you and I need to pray, spend time reading God's word, and to live out what we learn.

Of course, growing takes time. One of the best ways to grow is to learn from the strengths and the mistakes of those around us. In this chapter, we will dive into conversations about mental, physical, and spiritual growth so that, like a redwood tree, you will grow and accomplish what God has fashioned you to do!

Conversation #111

What things are you doing to develop your physical strength? Is there anything that you need to add to this list?

Conversation #112

What are you doing, or what could you do, to grow your friendships this year?

Conversation #113

What are some new things that you are currently learning? Do you enjoy learning? Why, or why not?

Conversation #114

What life lessons is your family learning right now? Are these lessons easy or hard for you?

Conversation #115

Do you think that it's always important to be learning and growing? Why, or why not?

Conversation #116

What types of things do you do, or will you do, to be a life-long learner?

Conversation #117

Do you know of anyone who is especially good at learning? What does this person do to keep growing? How could you model these qualities in your own life?

Conversation #118

Do you consider yourself a healthy eater? Why, or why not? What are some small things you could do to improve your eating habits?

Conversation #119

What are 1-2 bad habits that you would like to eliminate from your life? What steps will you take to get rid of these harmful habits?

Conversation #120

What are some good habits that you would like to add to your life? How will you start developing these positive habits? When will you start?

Friendship Conversations

A friend who understands your tears is much more valuable than a lot of friends who only know your smile.

~ Anonymous

Your family and your friends are the two groups of people who will influence you the most. In Seminary, the Hebrew language class was one of the most challenging courses I took. It was much more difficult than high school Spanish class.

It is also a course where I excelled. I owe a lot of this to my friends. Every Thursday, a group of us would meet in the mall food-court and study for hours. On the days I felt overwhelmed, frustrated, and wanted to quit, I had a group of friends cheering me on. My friends help me to succeed, and their encouragement made all of the difference!

Yet, friendships can also bring us down. Years later, when I worked as a therapist, part of my job was visiting youth in juvenile hall—a type of jail for kids. I would ask the teens I visited to tell me their story about getting locked up.

Usually, the story would begin with the words, "My friends and I..." Our friendships lead us to success or to disaster. It all depends on the types of friends that we allow into our lives.

Good friends hold us accountable for doing what is right. They lift us up to a higher level. When Jesus sent out His disciples to preach, He sent them out in pairs. Jesus knows the power of teamwork and friendship!

In this chapter, you will discuss the power of friendship with conversations that center around choosing and being the right type of friend.

Conversation #121

Who is your best friend, and how did you meet?

Conversation #122

What is it that makes your best friend so unique?

Conversation #123

What is one happy memory that you had with a good friend in the past week?

Conversation #124

What advice would you give to someone who wants to become a better friend?

Conversation #125

What are the most essential qualities of a good friend, and why?

Conversation #126

How do you know when a friend is a bad influence on you? Do you have any friends who are a negative influence on you right now?

Conversation #127

What have you done to be a good friend this week?

Conversation #128

Proverbs 18:24 says, "A man who has friends must himself be friendly" (NKJ). How are you friendly to others?

Conversation #129

Do you feel like it is easy or difficult for you to make new friends? Why?

Conversation #130

What are the most important things that good friends need to know about you?

Continuing the Conversation

It takes wisdom to love well!

~ *Jed Jurchenko*

Congratulations on completing this book! As we have seen, conversations matter It is amazing how much we learn about our friends and family when we take the time to ask.

Yet, finishing this book is only the beginning. You and your family are always changing. You will be different tomorrow than you are today, and your family will change too. Because of this, keeping the conversations going is necessary.

You may want to save this book and work through it again in the future. You might surprise yourself with how differently you see things over time. This very last question — number 131 — is all about exploring how you and your family will continue the fun, engaging, and creative conversations in the days ahead!

Conversation #131

What was your favorite part about working through this book? Now that you have completed these 131 conversations, how will you keep the conversations alive in your family?

About The Author

Jed Jurchenko is a husband, father to four girls, a psychology professor, and therapist. He is passionate about helping weary Christ-followers lead their families, grow their friendships, and caffeinate their faith so that they can live joy-filled Christ-honoring lives!

Jed graduated from Southern California Seminary with a Masters of Divinity and returned to complete a second master's degree in psychology. Jed and Jenny also enjoy walking on the beach, reading, and spending time together as a family.

Staying Connected

Let's stay connected! Coffee and conversation are two of my favorite things. I would enjoy hearing from you. Here are some additional ways to keep in touch with Jenny and me as well as ways to stay updated on all of the latest Coffee Shop Conversations happenings:

E-mail: jed@coffeeshopconversations.com

Twitter: @jjurchenko

Facebook: Coffee Shop Conversations

Blog: www.coffeeshopconversations.com

Thumbs Up
or Thumbs Down

THANK YOU for purchasing this book!

I would love to hear from you! Your feedback not only helps me grow as a writer, but it also helps me to get books into the hands of those who need them most. Reviews are one of the most significant ways that independent authors — like me — connect with new readers.

If you loved the book, could you please share your experience? Leaving feedback is as easy as answering any of these questions:

- What did you like about the book?
- What is your most crucial takeaway or insight?
- What have you done differently — or what will you do differently because of what you have read?
- Whom would you recommend this book to?

Of course, I am looking for honest reviews. So if you have a minute to share your experience, good or bad.

I look forward to hearing from you!

Sincerely,

COFFEE SHOP CONVERSATIONS

More Family Books

This book and other creative conversation starters are available at www.Amazon.com.

Transform your relationship from dull and bland to inspired, passionate, and connected as you grow your insights into your spouse's inner world! Whether you are newly dating or nearing your golden anniversary, these questions are for you! This book will help you share your heart and dive into your partner's inner world.

More Family Books

These creative conversation starters will inspire your kids to pause their electronics, grow their social skills, and develop lifelong relationships!

This book is for children and tweens who desire to build face-to-face connections and everyone who wants to help their kids to connect in an increasingly disconnected world. Get your kids talking, with this activity book the entire family will enjoy.

67386791R00057

Made in the USA
Columbia, SC
26 July 2019